Dodge Spring Special pickup (U.S.A., 1953)

Volkswagen Model 261 pickup (Germany, 1960)

Citroën HZ delivery truck (France, 1951)

Chevrolet Bison diesel truck (U.S.A., c. 1976)

Labatt's Streamliner (Canada, 1948)

Sentinel diesel DV46T coal dump truck (U.K., 1955)

THIS TRUCK

Paul Collicutt

Farrar Straus Giroux • New York

This book is for Ben from Uncle Paul

Copyright © 2004 by Paul Collicutt
All rights reserved
Distributed in Canada by Douglas & McIntyre Ltd.
Color separations by Hong Kong Scanner Arts
Printed and bound in the United States of America by Phoenix Color Corporation
Typography by Jennifer Crilly
First edition, 2004
1 3 5 7 9 10 8 6 4 2

Library of Congress Cataloging-in-Publication Data
Collicutt, Paul.
    This truck / Paul Collicutt.— 1st ed.
        p.   cm.
    Summary: Simple text and illustrations present different types of trucks and the work
they do.
    ISBN 0-374-37496-1
    1. Trucks—Juvenile literature.   [1. Trucks.]   I. Title.

TL230.15.C64 2004
629.224—dc21

                                                                                2002192896

This truck is small.

This truck is big.

This truck is enormous.

This truck flattens down the road.

This truck builds up a hill.

This truck crawls through the desert.

This truck races through the city.

This truck collects mail.

This truck delivers gasoline.

This truck is towing a boat.

This truck is carrying a rocket.

This truck has a short crane.

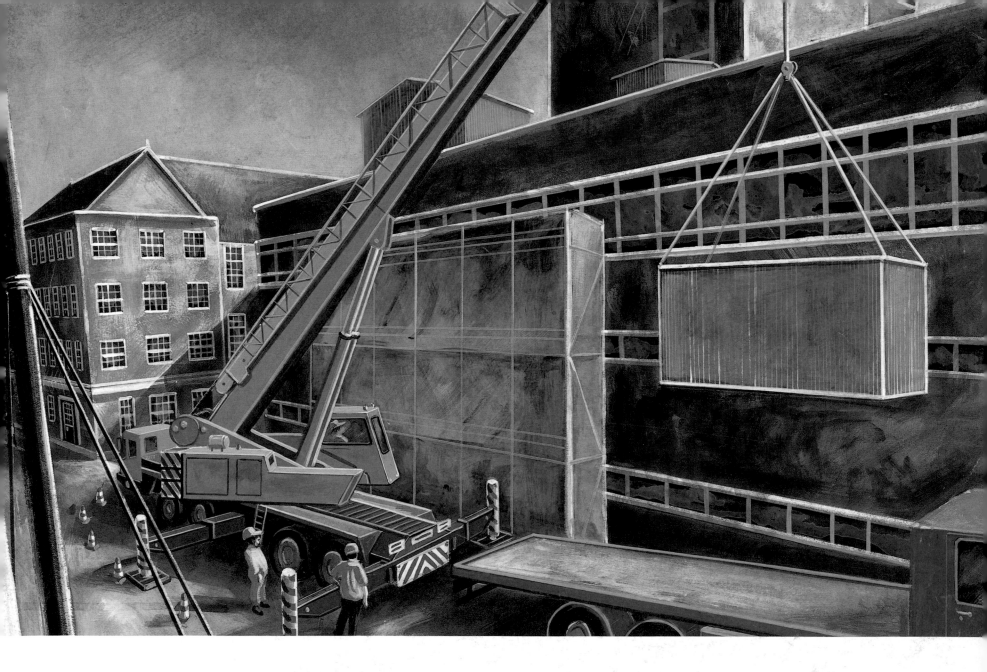

This truck has a long crane.

This truck pours out salt.

This truck sweeps up litter.

This truck travels all alone.

This truck travels in a convoy.

This truck picks things up.

This truck dumps things out.

This truck is overloaded.

This truck has no load at all.

This truck is all packed up,

ready to hit the road.

Caterpillar mining motor grader (U.S.A.)

Peterbilt 357 transfer dump truck (U.S.A.)

Garbage truck

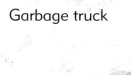

Decorated truck (Nepal)

Oshkosh HEMTT (heavy expanded
mobility tactical truck) (U.S.A.)

Ford Big Foot 4 x 4 "Monster Truck" (U.S.A.)